George Matheson

Words by the wayside

George Matheson

Words by the wayside

ISBN/EAN: 9783741132353

Manufactured in Europe, USA, Canada, Australia, Japa

Cover: Foto ©Andreas Hilbeck / pixelio.de

Manufactured and distributed by brebook publishing software (www.brebook.com)

George Matheson

Words by the wayside

Words by the Wayside

By George Matheson, M.A., D.D., F.R.S.E., Minister of the Parish of St. Bernard's, Edinburgh.

NEW YORK: BONNELL, SILVER & CO.,
24, West Twenty-second Street. 1896.

Contents.

	PAGE
The Goal of Spiritual Rest...	1
Varieties in Divine Selection	6
Things that Did Not Happen	11
The Leading of God...	16
The Influence of the Final on the Opening Chapter	21
The Test of Love's Genuineness	26
The Test of Love's Permanence	31
The Earlier and the Later Song	36
The Relation of Christianity to Pride...	41
An Unprepared Inhabitant of Heaven	46
The False Promise of Wealth	51
Love in Despair	56
A Noble Cowardice	61
The First Christian Union	65
The Three Humilities	69

CONTENTS.

	PAGE
The Wise Men and the Shepherds...	74
The Most Enduring Thing...	79
The Illumination of Faith...	84
Compassion for the Divine Cross...	88
The Ascent of Man...	93
Strength in Sorrow...	97
An Easter Meditation	101
Earthly and Heavenly Sorrow	106
Christian Fellowship...	110
The Double Source of Christian Fellowship...	115

Words by the Wayside.

The Goal of Spiritual Rest.

"He set my feet upon a rock, and established my goings."—PSALM xl. 2.

WHAT a strange contradiction—rest and movement, fixedness and pliability, steadfastness and variation. When we read the words, "He set my feet upon a rock," we think of a breathless calm; a rock is the symbol of rest. But we are startled when the psalmist adds, "He hath established my goings." How can a man be made to run by his fixedness? How can his power of motion be increased by that which is supposed to rivet him to the spot? In all things of the spirit, is it not ever so? Is not the rapidity of my movement always in proportion to the rootedness of my conviction? The firmer is my rock, the more established are my goings. It is the resting soul which flies. I have no wings until I have a fixed heart. The dove that descends upon the Jordan must first light upon the Son of Man. Is it not written, "They that wait upon the Lord shall renew their strength; they shall mount, they shall run, they shall walk"? What is that but to say that the rock makes the outgoing? I never do such work as when I am at rest. From the still, small voice of my heart come the thunder and the earthquake and the fire. It is the calm within makes the power without. The soul whose works have followed it is the spirit of the man who has rested from his labours.

Rock of Ages, within whose magic cleft my spirit would fain repose, it is not to shun the strife that I come to Thee. It is not to rest from labour that I would nestle under Thy shadow; it is that I may be "established in my goings." I come to Thee for wings—for new power of flight. I seek Thy rest because without Thee I cannot soar. I want to walk in the paths of righteousness, but I must first lie down in the green pastures. If my soul is troubled, I cannot journey; in vain shall the body travel if the mind has no rest. The road soon wearies my feet if something has not refreshed my soul; for it is by the soul, and not by the feet, that I make my way. Therefore, before I start, I want a rest in Thee. I want a golden gleam ere I touch the dusty plain. I want a draught of love ere I seek the sultry day. I want a strain of music ere I hear the wheels of earthly commerce. I want the spray of the fountain ere I meet the play of the passions. Only on the bosom of the Father shall I ride upon the wings of the wind. If I sleep, I shall do well. If my heart shall repose, my strength shall be wakened. One minute of heaven shall equip for all the years of earth. Rock of Ages, rest me ere I go.

Varieties in Divine Selection.

"Jesus loved Martha, and her sister, and Lazarus."—JOHN xi. 5.

THERE are three types of the Christian life—to do, to be, and to suffer. Martha is the type of action; she serves the table. Mary is the type of being; she sits at the feet. Lazarus is the type of suffering; he bears the Shadow of the Valley. All these are admitted into one guild—the love of Jesus. There are lives that come into the world to do; they are souls of great deeds; they leave their mark on time. There are lives that come into the world simply to be; they do nothing great; their presence is alone their shining. There are lives that come into the world to bear; their cross is itself their labour; they work by carrying. Christ has a home for all; nay, He has all in one home. There is no monotony in the kingdom of our Father. In the kingdoms of earth there is little room either for Mary or Lazarus; Martha has the best of it, nearly the whole of it. Often have I felt my life to be useless, aimless. There have been hours in which I have been forced to be Mary and Lazarus in one— just to be and to bear. I have rested on the couch of pain; I have missed my chance of promotion; I have seen the tide go out and leave me on the strand; I have cried in my despair, "To what purpose is this waste?" Be still, my soul; Mary and Lazarus are on the strand beside thee, Martha is but *one* of God's agents. There are moments in which thy Father is best served by silence. There are days which seem to live only for their beauty; they are windless, waveless, outwardly resultless; but they are numbered in God's year; they are loved like Mary. There are nights which seem to live only for their darkness; they are rayless, cheerless, preventing movement; but the unseen stars are all the time gliding through them; they are loved like Lazarus. Say not, in thy silent hour, that thou hast no mission. Had the Son of Man no mission? He said that His father had sent Him. Yet I think He was sent to the strand when the tide was out. He let Martha ride on the wave and He loved her; but He Himself stood on the shore with Mary and with Lazarus. His mission was to be and to bear. Christ and Him crucified, being and suffering, the flower and the thorn—these are His watchwords to-day. He has come up with Martha by the road of Mary, by the road of Lazarus. Remember it, oh my soul. Remember it on the shore from which thy wave has receded. Remember it on the bed where thy strength has become low. Remember it in the hour when the world has passed thee by.

Thy Gethsemane seems off the line; it has only the flower and the thorn. But one day there shall be no place as crowded in all the world. The city of God shall be built on the field of thy loneliness; where Mary and Lazarus are, Martha soon shall be.

Things that Did Not Happen.

"Anoint the shield."—ISAIAH xxi. 5.

WHAT is a shield? It is a very peculiar part of God's armour. It is not a strength in calamity; it is something which prevents calamity from coming. My strength is my power to bear; but my shield is my escape from bearing. My strength lifts me when the blow falls; my shield catches the blow before it falls. My strength supports what *is;* my shield wards off what might have been. I have often praised God for the

strength; but I have seldom
anointed the shield. I have recognised a thousand times His
songs in the night; but I have
not sufficiently thanked Him that
the night itself has not been
deeper. We are told that there
are "ships that pass in the night"
—golden opportunities that have
been lost in the darkness. And
doubtless there have been such.
But, I think, the large majority
of the ships that pass in the night
are not ships of gold. I am convinced that the vast proportion of
the opportunities that escape us
in the darkness are opportunities
not of gain, but of loss. There is
not one sea, however troubled, in
which I have not discovered a ship
that passed in the night—a ship

that was bearing trouble greater
still. I have read that in Gethsemane the Son of Man received
strength at the end; yes, but He
received a shield at the beginning.
"The cup which My Father hath
given Me, shall I not drink it?"
In the midst of His sea He saw a
ship of trouble that had passed in
the night. This cup might have
come *without* His Father; it might
have been an accident, a chance, a
contingency. He had been shielded
from that, and He anointed the
shield. He forgot the thought of
the present sea in the thought of
the ship that had passed by. He
accepted the night for the sake of
its one star; He took the cup from
His *Father*.

Oh, Thou Divine Man, let me

anoint the shield with Thee. Let me mark the blows that have not fallen; let me count the ships that have not come. When I am oppressed and weary I would always hear a voice saying, "You have not yet resisted unto blood." I am always forgetting the manna when I review my wilderness; I see not the bright light in the cloud, nor the shade that might have been deeper. Teach me to anoint my shield. Tell me of the arrows that were broken before they fell. Show me the pitfalls that my feet passed by. Light me to the darkness which my eye did not meet. Let me see the disappearing sail of the sorrow that has missed me. Guide me to the path of dangers unborn, of tears unshed, of cries unspoken. Let me gaze on the unwinged lightning; let me hear the unuttered thunder; let me read the page that was not suffered to be written. When I am in perplexity lead me to the valley that is lower than I. I shall worship Thee in my sorrow when I can worship behind the shield.

In the early part of this 32nd[?] / singer is making confession / of his sin & of his faith. And / suddenly / voice of G. is suffered / to break in upon / song, saying:

The Leading of God.

"I will guide thee with Mine eye."
PSALM xxxii. 8.

WHAT a frail thread of guidance for a human soul! A glance of God's eye—it seems a trivial thing. Why not a pressure of God's hand, a support of God's arm, a binding of God's golden chain? Does not He guide other things much more imperatively? Has He not bound the stars with an iron belt of law? They cannot, if they would, transgress. They keep their march unbroken, their step unflagging, their rhythm unwearied. But my soul has no belt around it. There is nothing which *compels* it to keep within its orbit. It can break away if it will; it has broken away many times. It has only the glance of God's eye, not the driving of His hand; only His direction, not His force, to guide. Wherefore is it so? Is not my soul of more value than many stars? Is it not more excellent in dignity, more wonderful in complexity, more beautiful in variety? Is it not a deeper note in the music of existence than all the harmony of the orbs of light? Why has it merely the guidance of the eye?

Just because it is *meant* to be a deeper harmony. What is it that makes thy life an intenser note than the music of the stars? Is it not just the fact that thou art free, just the circumstance that there is no iron belt around thee? What is this marvellous thing thou callest thy will? Wherein does its glory differ from the glory which the heavens declare? Is it not just in this, that thou art not *compelled* to come in? There is a guidance for thee, but it is not a star's guidance; it is a guidance of the eye. It is the only guiding which a will can get without dying. Wouldst thou be driven like a star? then must thou cease to be free. The heavens declare God's glory; but it is the glory of His hands. Who shall declare the glory of His Spirit? Not a star however bright, not a pulseless thing however fair; only something that can throb and strive and choose. He will not guide thee by aught but His eye. He will not *compel* thee to bear His cross. He will not sacrifice the joy of being loved to the pride of being obeyed. He will not allow thee to have only one tree in the garden. He is afraid to be accepted merely because there was no choice. The rivers of paradise run in their courses because they cannot get away. Not thus would He make *thy* paradise, oh my soul! He would surround Himself with rivals in thy heart. He would give thy steps room to stray. He would suffer thee to be led into temptation. He would show thee the

kingdoms of the world and the
glory of them. He would be loved
after experience; He would be,
not the inevitable, but the chosen,
one. He will not walk in the
garden until the cool of the day—
until thou hast had thy chance of
seeing life without Him. He will
draw thee, but He will never drive
thee; He shall guide thee only
with His eye.

The Influence of the Final on the Opening Chapter.

"I am the first and the last."
REVELATION i. & ii.

WHEN an artist sets to work on a picture, the first thing he sees is the last touch. The end exists in his mind before the beginning; the root comes after the flower. He never would begin his work if he did not first behold its finish. It is the completed form that moves him. He gazes on the summer while it is yet spring. It is not too much to say that his first is produced by his last. Through the gloom there glitters the glory. His eye rests not on the foundations; if it did, he would stop in disgust, abandon in despair. He sees nothing but the goal. Across the blots and blemishes there gleams the finished face —the face without a flaw. He is inspired by things not seen as yet. It is the light of to-morrow that leads him through the clouds of to-day; the last is the first.

And so, my Father, is it with Thee. From the foundation of Thy world, from the outset of Thy picture, Thou hast seen the finished flower—the sacrificial human soul, "the Lamb slain." For the sake of the flower Thou has planted the root. Thou wouldst not have fixed the root if Thou hadst not beheld the blossom. The Son of Man has been all along Thy atonement for the world. He has reconciled Thee to the days of chaos. He has reconciled Thee to the darkness on the face of the deep. He has reconciled Thee to the things without form and void. He has reconciled Thee to the alternate evenings and mornings that make up the day. He is Thy seventh morning, Thy Sabbath of rest. When Thou laidst the foundations of the earth, it was not on them that Thy gaze was reposing; it was on Him. When Thou saidst "Let us make man," it was not Adam that stood before Thee; it was He. The garden that was planted in Eden was a garden in Thy heart. Earth was not ripe for it. The soil was not prepared for it. Man was not fit to till it. When Thou wert walking in Thy garden in the cool of the day, the man seen by Thee was the coming man—the Man Christ Jesus. It was the ideal of Him, the coming of Him, that sustained Thy heart. The root was accepted for the sake of the flower. The river that made glad Thy city was none of the four that watered the earthly ground; it was the sight of an approaching life that would run into the ocean of Thy love. By the banks of that coming river the steps of Thy heart have ever wandered. It rippled in Thy spirit long ere it sounded in Thine ear. Thou wouldst have repented to have made man but for the rhythm of that river. Thine has been the artist's joy—the joy of the hour unborn, the joy of the day undawned, the joy of the beauty unreached, the joy of the light that is to be. Thou hast moved to the march of future music. Thou hast guided the world by the glow of its latest sun. The Man that came in the fulness of the years was the form that brooded on the face of the waters.

The Test of Love's Genuineness.

"Love rejoiceth not in iniquity."
1 CORINTHIANS xii. 6.

Is not that a strange thing to say? Is it not to praise love for something very inadequate? Why should true love have any temptation to rejoice in iniquity? Because there is a false love which does. There is an imitation of the real coin which is only proved to be spurious by this one mark of difference. There is a love which would like to be loved alone. It would rather have no competing object near it. It wants to stand

LOVE'S GENUINENESS.

in the foreground—to have the eye of the desired one rest on none but itself. And, to compass this aim, it would fain disparage all around it. It would rather that others fell back in the moral scale. It is glad to hear of that which detracts from them. It is cheered to find a stain on their garment. It is eager to propagate a rumour to their disadvantage. It is anxious that all should see their blemish —specially that the desired one should see it. It would be mortified to hear of a great deed which they had done; it rejoices in their iniquity.

My soul, is this true love in thee? Throw down the coin and see how it rings. Thou hast a love towards an earthly being;

what is the test of it? Should not love wish for its object the largest possible esteem, the widest circle of admirers? Should it not long before all things that its own verdict shall be confirmed by the universal voice? Should it not desire the time when its own vision of beauty shall become the common vision? Why should it be a joy to thee that the horizon of thy beloved is so limited? Why should it be a cheer to thee that he has so few to delight in? Why should it be a gladness to thy heart that others are not good enough to respond to his? Awake, my soul, thy coin will not ring; it is not true gold; it is not the love of thy Lord. Did *He* wish to shine before the Father by reason of surrounding iniquity? Listen: "that we all may be one as Thou art in Me." His greatest pain was His pre-eminence—His exclusive worthiness to be loved; it was His solitude, it was His cross. He was weary of the top of the hill and of the iniquity that placed Him there. He was jealous for the fame of His Father. He wanted Him to be appreciated, recognised, glorified. He wanted the one voice to be turned into a multitude, the one heart to be expanded into a universe. He bewailed the darkness that made His star so bright. He wept for the deformity that made His face so fair. He deplored the surrounding barrenness that enhanced His bloom. He was sad to be the chief among ten thousand. He wanted the kingdom to be taken by violence that His preciousness might become a common thing. He desired that His crown should be unmarked amid the crowd. He could not say, "I thank Thee that I am not as other men"—He mourned that other men were not like Him. He loved too deeply, to rejoice that He alone was worthy to be loved.

The Test of Love's Permanence.

"Because iniquity shall abound, the love of many shall wax cold."
MATTHEW xxiv. 12.

IT is not [merely] apostacy that is spoken of; it is the paling of the first fire. It is a sad thing that love should wax cold, that the old bloom should go off the flower, that the rose of morn should fade at midday. And yet I may torment myself wrongly on this account. I am often distressed about the failure of my heart when it is only the failure of my atmosphere. I am often languid because the air is heavy, dull because the mercury is low. I am effusive under the sky of Italy, undemonstrative in the fog of London. (I am elated to-day when there is much cause for weeping, depressed to-morrow when there is every ground for joy.) The rate of my own pulse quickens or retards the movement of the universe. Nor dare I say that my love declines because my *emotion* grows dim. Is it not a truth of life that active benevolence increases as passive sentiment subsides? Yon surgeon, who paces the wards with iron step, and surveys the wounds with unquivering eye, was once a youth fainting in pity at the sight of blood. Is he less pitiful now because he is more helpful? Is the love of humanity grown dim because it has ceased to express itself in sighs and tears? Is the heart less tender because it has more nerve? Is it a callous thing to be calm, ministrant, equal to the hour? (Is it a fading glow that shines no longer upon the hilltops but on dusky lane and wrangling mart? The bird that at morning perched upon a tree may light in the afternoon on the ledge of a warehouse wall. Is its plumage thereby less beautiful? Nay; neither is my love less fair because its song is less free.)

How, then, shall I know if my love grows cold? Our Lord answers, "By the deeds you do." "Because iniquity shall abound" —there is no test so sure as that.

My milestones are not in the air; they are on the dusty road. Can I read without tears that story of Calvary which once made me weep? Be it so; that is no proof of declining love. But have I gained facility in doing a mean thing, a heartless thing, an ignoble thing? Can I malign my brother to-day more easily than yesterday? Can I leap more nimbly the fence of forbidden things? Can I tread more airily the labyrinth of the crooked way? Can I repeat the *path* without the *pain* of wrong? Has the poison ceased to sicken me? Has the sting ceased to wound me? Has the arrow ceased to gall me? Has the sword ceased to smite me? Has the cloud ceased to blind me? Has the conscience ceased to upbraid me? Then, my soul, thou hast wandered; let thy Father lead thee home. Come out from the cold that benumbs thee. Come out from the painlessness that deceives thee. Come out from the sin whose penalty is that it smarts not. Come out into the scorching sun of God's judgment-day; and its heat shall make thee troubled, and by love's stripes thou shalt be healed.

The Earlier and the Later Song.

"My heart trusted in Him; and I am helped; therefore my heart greatly rejoiceth: and with my song shall I praise Him."—PSALM xxviii. 8.

THERE are two actions of the heart—prophecy and memory. In the morning of life I look forward, "my heart trusted"; in the afternoon I look back, "my heart rejoiceth." The morning trust comes before help; it is the prospect of the West seen from the crimson dawn. The afternoon joy follows help: it is the memory of the East seen from the setting sun. My heart is like the migration of the swallows. Every swallow makes its first migration in faith. It comes to seek a summer it has never seen. Who told it there were warm lands where it was going? It is an optimist before the fact; it journeys by faith. But when the swallow makes its second migration its prophecy is turned into a memory. It is no more the heart trusting, but the heart rejoicing. Its song has a new significance. It has been helped in the interval. It has crossed the boundary-line between instinct and experience. It has seen the summer of its dream.

My soul, which of thy migrations is the nobler? Is it the

trusting or the rejoicing, the prophecy or the memory, thy journey from East to West, or thy travelling from West to East? The Psalmist prefers thy evening song —the song of memory. Doubtless thy morning migration has its charm, the charm of instinctive hope, unconscious of the storm. But the very unconsciousness is the absence of perfect praise. Thy song of hope is thy song of youth. It migrates towards a summer unknown, and it praises as it goes. But it praises the goal, not the journey. All that lies between is so much waste—cloud and rain and cold. Thy father is blessed for thy coming Ararat, but not for the labours of thy wing. But thy song of memory is the song of age.

It has seen the summer and more; it has learned the weariness of the flight and the witheringness of the wind. Therefore its praise is precious to thy Father. It is no morning carol of the bird untried. It is rather the nightingale than the lark. It is the swallow after migration. It is a song *in spite of* storm. It is a praise of life as it *is*. Faith may sing of the rose behind the thorn; but love sits upon the rose bush and smiles back upon the thorn. Faith journeys from Egypt to seek the promised land; love rests in the promised land, and blesses the journey from Egypt. Faith vows all worship if it shall come without pain to the Father's house; love reposes in the Father's house and says: "It was good for me to have been afflicted." The song of memory is a song of praise.

The Relation of Christianity to Pride.

"I am not ashamed of the gospel of Christ; for it is the power of God."
ROMANS i. 16.

DR. WATTS says in one of his hymns that the cross of Christ has poured contempt on all his pride. Paul puts it rather differently. He says that the cross of Christ has not lessened his pride, but has lessened the sources of his humility—made fewer things to be ashamed of. Paul says that in entering into the life of sacrifice, the Christian is not passing into humility: he is wakening to the fact that something is dignified which he once thought mean. He once thought it was a mark of meanness to be a servant; he now finds it to be a mark of power—the very power of God. His pride has not stooped to the Gospel; it has embraced the Gospel. It has found a new channel for its exercise. It once deemed that its glory was to ascend; it is now proudest of descending. It once believed the goal to be a sceptre; it sees it now to be a cross. It once thought the majestic thing was to rule; it now finds that it is to serve. It was once ashamed to carry a parcel; it is now elated to wash a disciple's feet. It once felt the reproach of hands soiled by labour; it now craves the labour as the hand's jewelled ring.

My Saviour, I am not ashamed to come to Thee. I do not feel that my pride is taken down by coming to Thee. Rather, I seem for the first time to have found my dignity. Standing on the threshold of Thy service, I seem in the past to have been living below myself. My shame is not for *Thee;* it is for the days I have spent without Thee; I cry with Newman, "Remember not past years." Forbid that I should come to Thee like Nicodemus— by night. Let me have humility by all means, but let it be the humility of having been so long away from Thee, of having lost so many golden hours. Shall I be ashamed of loving *Thee,* of going where Thou goest, of dwelling where Thou dwellest? Shall I say that I have bowed my pride to serve *Thee?* Shall I dare to feel that I have condescended to follow *Thy* cross? Shall I speak of trampling on proud human nature when I come to *Thee?* Nay, my Lord, it cannot be. When I touch the hem of Thy garment I shall pour contempt, not on my pride, but on my past humility. I shall marvel at the contentment of my yesterday. I shall wonder that I was pleased with such small things. I shall be astonished at my little ambition, my poor aspiration, my mean estimate of the height of a human soul. Thy name shall be my boast. Thy love shall be my glory. Thy service shall be my birthright. Thy scars shall be my emulation. Thy burden shall be my kingdom. Thy pain shall be my palace. Thy cross shall be my crown. In the strength to bear Thy load I shall learn "the power of God."

An Unprepared Inhabitant of Heaven.

"Friend, how camest thou hither not having a wedding garment?"
MATTHEW xxii. 12.

THIS is a very peculiar picture. We see a sinful man who has passed successfully the gates of death and entered into the city of God. One would say his danger was now over. The problem with men has always been, "Shall we go to heaven or hell?" This man has solved that problem. He has gone to heaven. He has escaped even a purgatory. He has left all fires behind. He has been admitted into the traditional scene of rest.

And lo! his danger is only beginning. The real problem meets him within the vail. The question comes up in Paradise, "What shall I do to be saved?" He finds it was no good to get to heaven. It has not made him kin to the people there, has not lessened by a hairsbreadth the gulf between him and them. He does not wear their garment; their garment is love. He sees in heaven what he had pictured hell to be—a place of burdens. There is any amount of rapture, but it is over strange things. He sees admiring crowds, and he wonders what they admire. He hears exultant shouts, and he marvels that they come. The peace is to him dulness; the rest, vacancy; the joy, meaningless.

He had expected a holiday, and he finds a scene of work. He had looked for the death of care, and he sees care deepened. He had figured men with harps of gold rejoicing in the light of an unburdened day; and, behold! every man is bearing some human load, every heart waiting for the summons, "Enter ye into the pain of your Lord." The wedding garment has been dyed with blood.

My soul, why speakest thou of the solemnity of death? The solemn thing about thee is not that thou must die, but that thou must change. Imagine that there came to thee a strange message— that death was to pass thee by. If it were told thee that instead of the last sleep there would come to thee Elijah's chariot of fire, would it to thee be one whit less solemn? What shall become of thee when the fire-chariot lets thee down upon the hill of God? Is the hill of God thy atmosphere? What if the land should be a desert—desert to thee? What if there were no sign of communication between thee and its people—no possibility of such a sign? What if thy want should never be their want? What if the food that nourished them should leave thee hungry? What if their joys should be tasks to thee, their pastimes pains to thee, their hopes fears to thee, their loves aversions to thee? Thinkest thou it was written for nothing, "Enoch before his translation had this testimony, that he pleased God"? If thou art not in sympathy with the top of the universe, every step of the fire-chariot is a step of tragedy. Put on Christ ere thou leavest. Clothe thyself in love ere thou departest. Take the wings of the Spirit ere thou takest the wings of a dove. Robe thyself for heaven while yet on the shores of earth. Assume the garment of sacrifice, O, my soul.

The False Promise of Wealth.

"The cares of this world, and the deceitfulness of its riches."—MARK iv. 19.

WHY does our Lord call riches deceitful? The common answer is, "Because they take wings and flee away." What deceit is there in that? Did they ever promise to remain? Sometimes they do remain; but even then they have kept no promise. They have never professed to give joy for more than the hour; why call them deceitful? I do not think we have understood our Lord's meaning. He is not speaking of the *flight* of riches, but of their possession; not of their loss, but of their gain. He says that before they come they make a promise which they do not keep. They say that their advent will be the death of care. They predict the wings of an eagle to the man who gets them. They tell that the heart which holds them shall be light and buoyant, able to run and not be weary, to walk and not faint. And the moment they get into the hand they weigh it down. They break their pledge to the spirit. Instead of lifting care, they bring a new care. The birds lose their song. The colour of the rose is faded. The foot of the morning treads more heavily on the threshold. The laugh is less ringing, the step less springing, the heart less singing. The pulses do not beat so quickly to the old tunes. The march of the day tires us as it did not use to do. Sleep is more prized than waking, and, when the curtains of the West are drawn, our angel is wont to say, "Let me go, for the day breaketh."

My soul, the fault is not in the riches, but in their promise. Thou shouldst not have accepted that promise. It is not good to be free from care; it is not possible to be free. Thy choice is not between care and carelessness; it is between the cares of the world and the cares of God. It was deceit in riches to promise thee such freedom; it is not a man's freedom, it is not God's freedom. Wouldst thou be liberated from worldly care, it must be by another chain, albeit a golden chain. The cord of self can only be loosed by the cord of love. Did riches offer thee the open air? Then they offered what they could not give, what it would not be good for thee to receive. Not through the open air canst thou pass from thy prison-house. Not through the vacant field canst thou make thine escape from care. The door that lets thee out must lead into another prison-house; Christ must capture thee ere thy fetters fall. Not by laying thy burden down shalt thou be free; lift another's load and it shall drop from thy side. Add to the weight of thy ship by taking in the Son of Man, and its speed shall be so quickened that immediately it shall be at the land. Put your leprous hand to the cross to help Him up the Dolorous Way, and ere thou hast reached the top of the hill thou shalt seek its leprosy in vain. Thy care shall be cured by Calvary; the promise of thy Father shall never deceive thee.

Love in Despair.

"Then said Thomas: Let us also go, that we may die with Him."
JOHN xi. 16.

THIS is one of the most singular phases of faith in the whole Bible. Thomas is in absolute despair of Christ. He has lost belief in His power. He sees for Him nothing but the grave. He beholds no crown upon His brow. The vision of the kingdom has faded, and in its room there has come the shroud. To his mind there is nothing left for Jesus but to die. But now comes the remarkable thing. He is willing to take

Jesus at the lowest. Uncrowned, unseated, disrobed, he loves Him still. With the hosannas hushed, and the palm-leaves withered, and the crowds melted away, he loves Him still. His love has never been so full as now when his creed is empty. There have been men who have surrendered themselves to a Christ whom they believe to be King of kings and Lord of Lords. But here is a man who surrenders himself to a Christ whose kingdom he cannot see, and in whose lordship he has ceased to trust. Here is a man who has lost faith in Easter-day and believes only in Calvary, yet to Calvary he is willing to go. He will take the alabaster box after it is in fragments. He will take the manger without the star, the child without the angels, the cross without the crown. He will come to the Christ in the wilderness though there be no seraphs to minister to Him. He will seek the man in the garden, though there be no heavenly host to strengthen Him. He will break the bread of the Last Supper, though there be no promise of a feast above. He would rather have Christ with death than all the world beside with life eternal: "Let us also go that we may die with Him."

My soul, hast thou pondered this marvel of thy being? Paul says that thy hope and thy love shall abide together. Doubtless they shall. But there are

LOVE IN DESPAIR. 59

moments on earth in which thy love abides alone. To thee, as to Thomas, there come days in which hope deserts her sister. Thou callest them bad days, sceptical days, doubting days, days in which God has forsaken thee. Yet, sure I am that they are sent by Him. Thinkest thou it is not dear to thy Father that love betimes should stand alone? Thinkest thou it is not dear to thy Father that the eye should lose sight of the crown? There are songs of love which are songs in the night, and they are the most beautiful of all. They are the harp upon the willows, the strains by the waters of Babylon. They say: "Jesus, type of perfect beauty, I have wandered from all but Thee. I have lost the view of Thy kingdom, Thy power and Thy glory. I see no angel sitting on the gravestone; I catch no jubilant cry, 'He is not here.' But I bring my spices all the same. Hope's star may die, but it cannot rob me of my love. In the night my song shall be with Thee, oh Thou beautiful. I shall love Thee for Thyself when Pilate has disrobed Thee. I shall love Thee for Thyself when men have rent Thy garments. I shall love Thee for Thyself when despair has sealed a stone over Thy sepulchre. Rather than reign with Cæsar, I shall die with *Thee.*"

A Noble Cowardice.

"There is no want to them that fear Him."—Psalm xxxiv. 9.

This is often thought to mean that the man who fears God will have no struggle in life. That would not be true: and it would not be good if it were true; the road for the children of the Father has always been through the fire. Why, then, is it said "There is no want to them that fear Him"? It means that the fear of God does not indicate a defect of the nature. Blindness is a defect; deafness is a defect; lameness is a defect;

these all involve privation. But the fear of God does not involve privation; it implies possession. When I go into a picture gallery, and gaze on a work of some master, and say, "I fear I shall never come up to that," does that indicate want on my part? Nay, it is participation. It is the testimony that I am already an artist. My fear is the shadow of my love; the cloud into which I enter is born of my transfigured glory. I would not part with my cloud—not for sunbeams, not for worlds. It tells me that I have seen regions beyond. It is by the artist's soul that I know my own inartisticness; it is by the light of my rainbow that I see the flood. My night has come from day; it is not want that makes me fear.

Oh, Thou Divinely Beautiful, create within me the artist's fear. Give me the sense that I cannot come near Thee, that I am following afar off. Let me feel that Thou art in heaven and I on the earth. Let me tremble before Thy beauty—tremble with the impossibility of ever being worthy of Thee; let me begin to sink when I behold *Thee* on the waters. I am well content to sink if the weight that drags me down is the weight of Thy spirit. If I walk through the valley of the shadow, it is because Thou art with me. I could not feel the meanness of my apparel if I had not seen Thy bright raiment. I could not know the dimness of my candle if I had not gazed on Thy star. I could not learn the poverty of my dwelling if I had not lived in Thy palace. I could not hear the discord of my song if I had not listened to Thy music. My humility is my comfort. I am not proud of my rags, but I am glad of my power to see them. I could not have seen them had I not first seen *Thee*. It is by the light of Thy seamless robe that my tatters have been revealed to me. It is by the breath of Thy Spirit that I have learned with trembling what it is to be dead. My trembling is my triumph; my crouching is my crown; my day of judgment is my year of jubilee, for my cry has come from the taste of Thy glory, there is no want in them that fear Thee.

The First Christian Union.

"The crooked shall be made straight, and the rough places plain; and the glory of the Lord shall be revealed, and all flesh shall see it together."—ISAIAH xl. 4, 5.

AND so the union of Churches is to be a very late thing; God's glory is to be revealed before we are agreed about His doctrine. And what is God's glory? It is the ministration of love—"The crooked shall be made straight, and the rough places plain." We are not to wait for a union of *opinions;* we are to begin with a union of hearts. We are to be united, while yet we do not "see together." A thing may be revealed both to you and to me which yet we do not see together. You and I may look at the same stars and call them by other names. *You* are an astronomer, and *I* am a peasant; to you they are masses of worlds, to me they are candles in the sky set up to light me home. What matter? Shall we not enjoy the glory though we are not agreed about it? *You* speak of the law of Nature, and I of the will of God; but to each of us the word is written with a capital, and to both of us its message is the same. Let us join hands over the message ere we settle our dispute about the messenger; it is ever the voice in the wilderness, "Make the crooked straight, make the rough places plain." Ye who stand upon

the shore and wrangle about the
number of the waves, there is
meantime a work for you to do,
and to do together. There are
shipwrecked voyagers out yonder
who are crying and calling. They
have folded their hands in prayer,
and have heard no answer but the
echo of their cry. Say, shall they
call in vain? Shall they wait until
you have counted the billows that
consume them? Shall they stand
shivering in the storm while you
are disputing the name of the lifeboat? What matter how we name
the lifeboat if only we each believe
in it? Come out to the wreck, my
brothers. Come out where the
breakers are roaring, where the
foam is lashing, where the timbers
are creaking. Come out and reveal

the glory of the Lord, which is the love of man. Come to the souls that have lost their compass, to the lives that have broken their helm, to the hearts that have rent their sails. They will not ask the name of your lifeboat; even Jacob's angel had no name. You may not see together, but you shall reveal together—reveal the glory of God. You shall be the Church of united sympathisers. You shall hold your service at night—in the absence of clear vision. You shall not see together the face of the Master, but you shall touch together the print of the nails. Your bond for to-day shall be the aroma of the spikenard that anointed Him for burial; to-morrow, please God, you shall see Him as He is.

The Three Humilities.

"*What doth the Lord require of thee, but to do justly, and to love mercy, and to walk humbly with thy God.*"—MICAH vi. 8.

THE prophet begins at the top of the ladder, and steps downward. Let us begin at the foot, and go upward. You might think that the hardest of the three was to "walk humbly with your God." No; it is the easiest. It is no great task to be humble before *God*. What else can a frail mortal be, in the presence of One so far above him? Can he do otherwise than beat upon his breast, and cry "unclean"? But it is a harder thing to be humble before one who is my moral inferior—to "love mercy." When a man or woman has been a special sinner, and I am called to judge, it is very difficult to feel lowly, very difficult not to thank God that I am not as other men. But the hardest thing of all is to be humble when I meet my equal—to "do justly." When I come into rivalry with a man who is my match, what temptations I have to exalt myself and to bring him down! How I would like to feel that I am superior all round! How I try to prove that I am the taller man; how I rejoice in the sight of his shadow! I could easily be *generous;* if I thought his chances poor, I could say kind things. But, to be just, to bring myself down to him, to feel that he is as good as I, as worthy as I, to make allowance for his weak points in the light of my own, to admit the things in which he might stand above me—this is to triumph in Christ, this is the crown of glory.

Behold then, my soul, the ladder of thy humiliations—thy humility before God, thy humility in the presence of the fallen, thy humility in contact with thy rival. Thou shalt find them progressively hard; the first shall be the easiest of all. Therefore, my soul, I have a specific for thee; practise the first continually. In every contact with thy fellow-man, remember thy hour alone with God. When thy fallen brother stands before thee and thou art tempted to be proud, remember thy hour with God. When thy rival stands before thee and thou art constrained to vaunt thyself, remember thy hour with God. Remember that thou art still with God. Remember that thou hast never left that awful Presence where man has no temptation to be aught but humble. Remember, thou art still in His sight as fallen as the lowest, as worthless as the vilest, as polluted as the sinfulest. When thou art tempted to compare thy candle with another's taper, turn thy candle toward the sun, and it will go out. Set the Lord always before thee, and thou shalt never be moved — never moved from generosity, never moved from justice. Fix thine eye upon the sun, and thou shalt no more distinguish between the candle and the taper. See the King in His beauty, and thou shalt see thyself ever in deformity. Gaze on the spotless Lamb, and to thee there shall be no whiteness in all the world beside. Thou shalt climb the ladder of all humiliations if thou art walking ever with thy God.

The Wise Men and the Shepherds.

"There were shepherds abiding in the fields, keeping watch over their flock by night. And, lo! the angel of the Lord came upon them, and the glory of the Lord shone round about them."—LUKE ii. 8, 9.

WHAT a difference between the Christmas of the shepherds and the Christmas of the wise men. It is not the thing revealed that is different: it is the manner of its coming. The wise men got their Christmas greeting after hard work. They had to journey from the East; they had days of seeking, nights of walking, hours of weariness. But the shepherds got their Christmas card without seeking it. They were not straining their eyes toward the sky. They were thinking of something else. Their gaze was on the ground; they were engaged in homely work; they were keeping watch over their flock. And, all at once, unsought and unexpected, the light shone. What the wise men had seen after long struggle the shepherds beheld in a moment, in the twinkling of an eye. Whence this contrast? Can we account for it; can we explain it? Yes; very easily. It was just their attitude of mind that made the difference. The wise men were speculating, dreaming, thinking of nothing else, doing nothing else; they were so anxious about the

Star that they nearly missed it. But the shepherds were engaged in daily duty. They were performing the common round, the household task, the drudgery of the appointed hour. And, lo! while they were standing at the door, Christmas came in at the window. While they were doing the duty of earth, there flashed on them the glory of heaven. While they watched their flocks by night, there broke on them the angel of the day.

My soul, if thou wilt, even such may thy Christmas be. Its greeting would come to thee more easily if there were less intellectual strain. There is too much speculative outlook for the Star; that is the reason there is so little vision.

Art thou tormenting thyself with the wise men about advent doubts? Leave the wise men and go with the shepherds. Go out into the field to keep the flock; go into the night to guard the fold. Turn aside from the searching of the eye to the working of the hand. Pass from the seeking to the knocking. Forget the Star in the manger. It was when Mary "turned" that she saw Jesus. The strain of looking right before thee is hurtful to thy view. Turn aside, oh my soul. Turn to the help of the helpless; turn to the succour of the sad. Turn to bring your gold and frankincense and myrrh to the homes of poverty and pollution. And suddenly in the place thou hast blessed there shall be revealed a child Jesus, and through the once polluted air there shall float circumambient music, and in the scene of thy former night Christmas Day shall come.

The Most Enduring Thing.

"Love never faileth; but whether there be prophecies, they shall fail; whether there be tongues, they shall cease; whether there be knowledge, it shall vanish away."
1 Cor. xiii. 8.

THERE is a form of advice given by pastors and teachers at the New Year with which I have little sympathy. They tell us that such a time should remind us of the perishableness of earthly things. To me it reminds of the contrary —of the things which are not perishable. I think the marvellous element about the fleeting years is not what they take away, but what they leave behind. Paul seems to have felt this. To him the marvel was not that tongues should cease, nor prophets fail, nor knowledge vanish away, but that love should abide. And truly, that should be *our* marvel, our New Year lesson to the young and old. It is not fleeting things which make us feel solemn; it is those which are permanent. We are more solemn before the mountain than before the stream, because the mountain has a greater semblance of rest. But what shall I say of love—love that is the oldest and the youngest thing in the world—love which is timeless, yearless, dateless, endless? I shall say that to contemplate its changelessness is the solemn thought for every New Year. There is an object in this universe which the years sweep over in vain; it is the heart. All else within thee may faint and grow weary. Tongues may cease. The orator's voice gets thinner, and the singer's notes more shrill. Prophecies may fail. The man of business may lose his speculative foresight, and the statesman his predictive power. Knowledge may vanish away. The memory may become forgetful of much of the wealth it has gathered. But the heart, the heart—we must draw the line there. The heart is green in winter, it flowers amid the snow. It is independent of tongues; when the voice is too weak for speech, the soul can sing. It is independent of prophecy; when sight is too dim to pierce the cloud, faith can cry, "Oh, grave, where is thy victory?" It is independent of knowledge; when the laws of astronomy are forgotten, the starry mansions are visible to love. Take not, then, thy text from the fading leaf to-day. Thy years have left thee young, young in the inner man. Love has not improved since Ruth sang, "Entreat me not to leave thee." It was then in its morning; it is in its morning still. It stood upon Mount Ararat when life was young, and beheld, not the flood, but the rainbow; it stands upon Mount Nebo when life is old, and surveys still the Promised Land, and its eye is not dim, and its natural strength is not abated. Thou shalt meet thy first morning at the end of the years; heaven and earth shall pass away, but love faileth never.

The Illumination of Faith.

"The exceeding greatness of His power to usward who believe."
                            EPHESIANS i. 19.

I THOUGHT the power of God was most seen towards unbelievers. I thought it was the children of disobedience who felt the thunder, the earthquake and the fire. No; it is the reverse. Nobody can see the power of God from the outside. Nobody can see the power of anything from the outside. No man can be *led* into the art gallery by the power of art; to see its power he must come in. Would you know the power of Tennyson?

[handwritten note:] Do you want to see ? keenest sense of personal sin — go not where

Then you must read "In Memoriam"; it is only within the palace that the fire is burning. Not even against sin is the power of God best seen by the sinner. It is the good man that most feels the judgment of badness. One sting of conscience outweighs a hundred lightning-bolts. And conscience belongs to the good, ~~is at least a remnant of goodness.~~ That which feels remorse in me is the survival of the better man, or the birth of the new man. The books that shall be opened at the judgment-day shall be the heart's most unspotted leaves. The light which reveals our secret sins is the light of God's countenance.

Lord, let me in, that I may see Thee. I have been trying too

where) students chamber is still
&) holy man is on his knees;

long to judge Thee from the outside; let me in. I have asked my soul where is the sign of Thy power. I have asked what good there is in *being* good. I have asked what advantage the righteous have over the wicked. I have forgotten that the advantage can only be seen inside the door. I have forgotten that the poet may be threadbare and yet joyous, that the painter may be penniless and yet exultant. I have forgotten that the reward of art is beauty, that the reward of loving is being loved, that the reward of holiness is strength in temptation. I shall see Thy power within Thy holy place; in Thy light shall I see light. Lord, Lord, open unto me. Give me a view from within. Let me look at the outer grounds from the window of Thy dwelling. Let me gaze on Thy world from where Thou Thyself art standing. And I know that the prospect shall be changed, the crooked shall be made straight, and the rough places plain, and the glory of the Lord shall be revealed. I shall see Thy exceeding power when once I have believed.

Compassion for the Divine Cross.

"All kindreds of the earth shall wail because of Him."—REVELATION i. 7.

SOME one has defined religion to be "pity for God." It is a bold definition, but there is a side on which it is true. We are apt to think that the joy of our Lord is the only motive to religion. It is not so. I may be drawn to love by the pain as well as by the joy of the object. I am told that there is a Divine cross. Where can it lie? you say. Is not God exalted in majesty above all other beings? Yes, and that is just where it lies; the Divine cross is the Divine solitude. We commonly think of a king as the symbol of joy. I never do. To me the first sensation awakened by the name of King is that of pity. I see one whose life is led in an abiding loneliness—a loneliness which is rather enhanced than diminished by the crowds which surround Him. I heard a minister once pray for the Queen "in her lonely life." It suggested to me that singular passage, "Except a corn of wheat fall into the ground and die it abideth alone." It made me understand how the Divine pain rose out of the Divine greatness, how the crown itself became the cross. It gave a new significance to the old words which inspiration has heard on the lips of the Divine—"I thirst." The height of God's throne is the depth of God's solitude; the increase of His command is the lessening of His communion.

My soul, hast thou entered into the pity of that thought—the wailing over the cross of God? I have heard thee say, "God is sufficient unto Himself." He is not, or His name would not be love. Love means insufficiency to one's self; Divine love is most of all insufficient. What though He comes with clouds of majesty if the very majesty makes Him alone. The sword that pierces Him is thine absence from the scene of His glory; as He treads the wine-press there is none with Him. Say, wilt thou break through the cloud, oh, my soul? Wilt thou come to the heart of thy Lord? Still He carries His cross up the Dolorous Way, still He faints under His burden of loneliness. Renew thy past efforts, successful or vain. Bring Simon of Cyrene to bear, without compulsion, His cross. Bring Mary of Magdala to share His reproach for wasted tears. Bring Nicodemus to break the silent night in which He dwells. Bring the dying malefactor to remember *Him* in His kingdom. Bring the man that lay on Christ's bosom to rest Christ on *his* bosom. Bring Peter bar-Jona to watch with Him the missing hour. Often hast thou cried because thou needest Him: hast thou no voice of wailing because He needeth *thee?*

The Ascent of Man.

"O send out Thy light and Thy truth; let them lead me: let them bring me unto Thy holy hill, and to Thy tabernacles. Then will I go unto the altar of God, unto God, my exceeding joy."—PSALMS xliii. 3, 4.

THERE are five stages in the light of God. The first is simple leading — the guiding of a child. Then comes the height of ecstasy —the holy hill; I stand above the world and laugh at the cares of time. By-and-by comes a third stage; I descend from the hill to the tabernacles. Ecstasy subsides into peace; the height sinks into the home; love on the wing becomes love in the nest. After this comes the light of sacrifice —" Then shall I go unto the altar of God." "Then," not before. Peace alone can sacrifice for others. I cannot sacrifice when I am being led; I am thinking too much about my own steps. I cannot sacrifice when I am in ecstasy; I am too intent on my own joy. But when I get peace, I go out from myself altogether; I go to the altar. At last the climax comes. The altar itself becomes "my exceeding joy," not the joy of the hill, not the ecstasy of being removed from care, but the rapture of forgetting self in the care of another. The joy of God's altar is love.

To Thee, O Life Divine, from step to step I rise—through leading, through ecstasy, through peace, through sacrifice—up to Thy love, which is sacrificial joy. It is a spiral stair, but it is golden. Sometimes it seems to make no progress. There are moments when my feet grow weary with their climbing, and the end is not yet. Shine from the topmost height, Thou Divine Joy! Often I am led by a way which by myself I would not go; I see not the Christ, but only the manger. Shine out, Thou Christ, and the manger shall be luminous. Shine out, and the altar shall glow with the light of coming fires. Shine out, and the tabernacle shall no more seem a decadence from the hill-top. Shine out, and the days of leading shall themselves be days of light, cheered by an unknown prospect, sustained by a promise of exceeding joy.

Strength in Sorrow.

"God said, Let there be a firmament in the midst of the waters."—Genesis i. 6.

THAT has been the voice of God's providence through all ages, the desire to create a firmament "in the *midst* of the waters." The firmament of other religions has been at the *end* of the waters. There is no faith which has not hoped for a haven, no worship which has not promised its votaries a Sabbath of rest. But all other worships have made their votaries wait for their rest until the Sabbath has come. God promises His rainbow in the Flood, His firmament in the midst of the waters. "Thou hast enlarged me when I was *in* distress" is the surprised cry of the Psalmist; "the peace that passeth knowledge" is the surprised cry of St. Paul. And truly it is wonderful. That I should have a firmament in the midst of the waters, that I should be calm in the very heart of storm, is a marvellous thing. It is no marvel to believe in a *final* rest; even an atheist might do that. The very *torrent* of grief causes it to exhaust itself, and promises one day a great repose. But to have repose in the *midst* of the torrent, to have anchorage at the height of the storm, to have rest now, here, in the very scene of the flood—

STRENGTH IN SORROW.

this is Divine peace; this is the rest of God.

My soul, let no one rob thee of thy promise in Christ. They will tell thee that there is no difference between thy lot and other lots. Outwardly there is not. Thou and thy brother may be tossing on the same sea, grinding at the same mill, toiling in the same field; yet thine may be the firmament, and his only the waters. Thou mayest not escape the den of lions any more than he; but to thee the lions are dumb. It is not thy circumstances that are the measure of thy peace; it is thy peace that is the measure of thy circumstances. The sea that drowned Pharaoh became dry land to Moses. Thy firmament is within thee, oh, my soul! The force of the waters is not abated, but thy force is increased. The night is not less dark, but there is a new lens in thine eye. The weight is not less heavy, but there is a new strength in thine arm. The stroke is not less sharp, but there is a new shield on thy breast. The way is not less long, but there is a new spirit in thy feet. The message has not lost a word of its pain, but there is a new light in thy heart. Thou hast heard of the ram in the thicket, and the call to Mount Moriah is tearless. Thy firmament is in the midst of the waters.

An Easter Meditation.

"Made of the seed of David according to the flesh; and declared to be the Son of God with power, by the resurrection from the dead."—ROMANS i. 3, 4.

CHRIST had two risings; He rose from the seed of David, and He rose from the seed of death. He had a double Christmas. His first Christmas was His birth from the house of Israel; His second was His birth from what we call the narrow house appointed for all living. But the narrow house was the larger ancestry; His second Christmas was the more glorious. His first coming was, after all, from a very slender root—a small fragment of the race of man. But Easter Day was His true Christmas. It came from man himself—man at the lowest, and, therefore, man at the widest. We do not all sit in the house of David; but we all rest in the house of death. That is to me the charm of Easter Day. It is not simply that Christ ascended; it is that He ascended from our most hopeless state, our most universal state. There have been other visions of ascending souls. We have seen Enoch ascending; we have seen Elijah ascending. But even while we gaze, we are parted from them. We feel that their rising has not come from the common ground, the ground of our corruption;

there is a great gulf fixed between us. But when Christ rises we rise with Him. We feel that He has risen out of our dust, out of our miry clay. We see Him borne upwards on no impossible chariot of fire, but on the wings of our human weakness. We see Him ascend from no vanished stem of royalty, but from the meanest level of the lowliest soil. The possibility which Easter reveals is the possibility of death's own life.

And so, I can understand why it is written, "Come, see the place where the Lord lay." The place itself has received a promise. Nothing but Easter Day can make me put flowers upon my brother's grave. Not even Elijah's chariot could do that. That would be an immortality purchased by the *escape* of death. But Thou, O Lord, hast lighted my torch *within* the valley. Thou hast blossomed from my barren soil. Thou hast bloomed from the ground of my winter. Thou hast shone from the depth of my night. Thou hast smiled from the mist of my tears. It is with the key of death that Thou hast opened heaven; it is in the robes of my grave Thou hast found revival. Thou hast magnified my dust; therefore I deck it with flowers. I put *immortelles* on the grave to say that death is a delusion—to tell, not so much that it is conquered, as that it had no need to be conquered. Thou hast destroyed, not death, but death's deception; the resurrection from the dead is the message of Easter Day.

Earthly and Heavenly Sorrow.

"God divided the waters which were under the firmament from the waters which were above the firmament."—GENESIS i. 7.

YES, He divided the waters of trouble into two orders. He taught man to distinguish between two kinds of sorrow—a lower and a higher. Never forget that lesson. It was a lesson which the Jew was very slow to learn. When he saw a suffering man he concluded he must be a bad man. When he beheld Job afflicted, he said, "What evil has he done?" It never occurred to him that Job might have been afflicted because he was good. It never dawned upon him that there are waters above the firmament as well as waters under the firmament. Yet it is true. There is a sorrow which can only be felt in the upper air; it was the sorrow of the Son of Man. Men thought the Father could not have delighted in Him, or He would have taken Him down from the cross. It was because the Father delighted in Him that He did not take Him down. We often say that sorrow is for our good; sometimes it is not only *for* our good, but is itself our good. Think you that Christ's tears over Jerusalem could have come from any but perfect eyes? Think you that His grief in Gethsemane could have dimmed any but a spotless heart? Think you that His cry on the cross could have fallen from any but a stainless spirit? The waters of His trouble were above the firmament.

My soul, how shalt thou know to which class belong thy waters? Consider what divides the waters which are under the firmament from the waters which are above the firmament. It is the Spirit of God—the spirit of unselfishness. It is not whether thy sorrow be secular or sacred that makes the boundary line. Thy grief may be for the loss of worldly wealth, and yet it may be a grief above the firmament. For what art thou lamenting the loss of this wealth?

Is it because it would have gladdened somebody? Is it because it would have paid a poor man's rent or endowed a sick man's hospital? Is it because the want of it has crippled thee from doing good? Is it because it might have prevented Lazarus from lying at the gate and feeding on the accidents of fortune? Then thy grief is not earth-born; it cometh from on high; it has its home with God; it has its companionship with the angels; it is a travail of the soul with which Heaven itself can be satisfied, for the fountain of its waters is above the firmament.

Christian Fellowship.

"That which we have seen and heard declare we unto you, that ye also may have fellowship with us."—1 JOHN i. 3.

THE root of all fellowship is identity of mental vision—a seeing and hearing in common. There are some kinds of love which do not need this. A mother's love does not; it exists for her child when it sees and hears nothing, when it is life and no more. Charity does not; it is love in the dark, love in suspense of judgment. Mercy does not; it is love with a broken ideal, disappointed, but not dispelled, repining, yet refusing to give in, weeping the want of harmony, yet working for its object still. But fellowship cannot exist where harmony does not exist. It demands a common interest of the heart. There may be any other difference but that. There may be a disparity of age. There may be a contrast of manner. There may even be a difference of opinion; but a common subject of interest there must be. The companionship of the hearth and of the home, the companionship of the city and of the field, the companionship of the sick-room and of the study, must be based upon the things which you and I have seen and heard together.

Son of Man, give us a common

interest in Thee; it is the only thing that will make us one. Help us through a common love to forget our individual desires. It is my individual desires that make me a dull companion. Often in the social hour I sit silent, not because I am ignorant, but because I am uninterested. I am thinking of myself — my exchange, my counting-house, my workshop. Men tell me that Thy cross is meant to crucify the world in me. Yes, but the world in me is not my companionship, but my solitude. When Thou sayest "Love not the world," Thou sayest "Love not thyself." I am too much alone, too much with my own thoughts. I am abstracted at the marriage feast, I am listless in the

CHRISTIAN FELLOWSHIP.

scene of mirth, I do not kindle into warmth with the voices of the company. I am absorbed in the world—the world of my own soul. Crucify my world, O Christ! Crucify my spirit of isolation, my desire to be alone. Abolish my desert life, my walking in the wilderness. Give me power to come out from myself into the community of men, into the common love. Let me learn that to become unworldly is to become social; that to give up life's vanity is to give up life's solitude. Translate me from my garden into Thy city, from the place where I hide myself among the trees to the voices of that great multitude which no man can number. The world is within my own heart. When I have left the world I shall have fellowship with all.

The Double Source of Christian Fellowship.

"Truly our fellowship is with the Father, and with His Son Jesus Christ."
1 JOHN i. 3.

THE thought evidently is that the man who would commune with Christ must have a previous communion—a communion with the Father. Can you fail to see the reason? It is because the Divine in Christ can only be seen by a nature already kindred. Do you remember our Lord's joy over Simon's recognition—" Flesh and blood have not revealed it unto thee, but My Father which is in heaven." He felt that the man who had made such a discovery must already be in fellowship with something more than the common earth and sky. He felt that the Divine alone could have discovered the Divine, that the fellowship with the Son must have been preceded by the fellowship with the Father. Did you ever detect beneath the squalor of a ragged boy the marks of an aristocratic bearing? What did that detection prove? That the boy was aristocratic? Yes, but that you were, too. You could not have seen it but for your own bearing or the bearing of some of your ancestors far away. It is by your own light that you have seen his light; it is by your own dignity that you have perceived his dignity; you have testified to yourself in testifying to him.

And this, Thou Divine Man, is my comfort in recognising *Thee;* I must be like Thee when I have seen Thee as Thou art. I have seen Thee through the rags of the rent garment; I have seen Thee in Thy poverty and in Thy pain. Thou hast the form of a servant, yet I know Thee to be a King's son. Thou hast emptied Thyself of all majesty, yet I bow before Thee. Thou carriest a cross, yet I see on Thy head a crown. I have recognised Thee spite of Thy lowliness, spite of the thorns with which they have wreathed Thy brow. Whence have I recognised

Thee, O Lord? Not by flesh and blood. Thy flesh is more marred than the sons of men; Thy blood is poured out in death. To the carnal eye Thou art a failure; it sees no beauty that it can desire in Thee. Whence have I recognised Thee? Surely because there is a cord between us somewhere. Surely because Thy Father is my Father. Thou comest to me not merely as a hope, but as a memory. Thou art not a stranger to me. I have heard the song before. Where? Was it when heaven lay about me in my infancy, or when my childhood saw wonder in the cloud? I cannot tell. I only know that a mirror within me has been waiting for Thy light, and that the music of Thy voice is an echo of long ago. He that has seen Thee must have first seen the Father.

www.ingramcontent.com/pod-product-compliance
Lightning Source LLC
Chambersburg PA
CBHW022141160426
43197CB00009B/1389